A NOTE ON BOOKBINDING
BY DOUGLAS COCKERELL

WITH EXTRACTS FROM THE SPECIAL REPORT OF THE SOCIETY OF ARTS ON LEATHER FOR BOOKBINDING

Copyright © 2018 Read Books Ltd.
This book is copyright and may not be
reproduced or copied in any way without
the express permission of the publisher in writing

British Library Cataloguing-in-Publication Data
A catalogue record for this book is available from
the British Library

A History of Bookbinding

Bookbinding, at its simplest, is the process of physically assembling a book from a number of folded or unfolded sheets of paper or other material.

Before the computer age, the bookbinding trade involved two divisions. First, there is stationery or vellum binding which deals with making new books intended to be written into, such as accounting ledgers, business journals, and guest log books, along with other general office stationery such as note books, manifold books, portfolios, etc. Second is letterpress binding which deals with making new books intended to be read from, and includes fine binding, library binding, edition binding, and publisher's bindings. Today, modern bookbinding is divided between hand binding by individual craftsmen versus mass-produced bindings by high speed machines in a bindery factory.

The craft of bookbinding probably originated in India, where religious sutras were copied on to palm leaves (cut into two, lengthwise) with a metal stylus. The leaf was then dried and rubbed with ink, which would form a stain in the wound. The finished leaves were given numbers, and two long twines were threaded through each end (through wooden boards), making a palm-leaf book. When the book was closed, the excess twine would be wrapped around the boards to protect the manuscript leaves. Buddhist monks took the idea through Persia, Afghanistan, and Iran, to China in the first century BCE. Similar techniques can also be found in ancient Egypt where priestly texts were compiled on scrolls and books of papyrus.

Writers in the Hellenistic-Roman culture wrote longer texts as scrolls; these were stored in boxes or shelving with small cubbyholes, similar to a modern wine-rack. Court records and notes were written on wax tablets, while important documents were written on papyrus or parchment. The book, as we know it today was not needed in ancient times, as many early Greek texts (scrolls) were customarily folded accordion-fashion to fit into the hand. In addition to the scroll, wax tablets were commonly used as a writing surface. Diptychs and later polyptych formats were often hinged together along one edge, analogous to the spine of modern books, as well as a folding concertina format. Such a set of simple wooden boards sewn together was called a codex (pl. codices) by the Romans – from the Latin word caudex, meaning 'the trunk' of a tree.

Western books from the fifth century onwards were bound between hard covers, with pages made from parchment folded and sewn on to strong cords or ligaments that were attached to wooden boards and covered with leather. Since early books were exclusively handwritten on handmade materials, sizes and styles varied considerably, and there was no standard of uniformity. Early and medieval codices were bound with flat spines, and it was not until the fifteenth century that books began to have the rounded spines associated with hardcovers today. Because the vellum of early books would react to humidity by swelling, causing the book to take on a characteristic wedge shape, the wooden covers of medieval books were often secured with straps or clasps. These straps, along with metal bosses on the book's covers to keep it raised off the surface that it rests on, are collectively known as 'furniture'.

Luxury medieval books for the library had leather covers decorated, often all over, with tooling (incised lines or patterns), blind stamps, and often small metal pieces of furniture. Medieval stamps showed animals and figures as well as the vegetal and geometric designs that would later dominate book cover decoration. Until the end of the period, books were not usually stood up on shelves in the modern way. The most functional books were bound in plain white vellum over boards, and had a brief title handwritten on the spine. Techniques for fixing gold leaf under the tooling and stamps were imported from the Islamic world in the fifteenth century, and thereafter the gold-tooled leather binding has remained the conventional choice for high quality bindings for collectors.

Although the arrival of the printed book vastly increased the number of books produced in Europe, it did not in itself change the various styles of binding used, except that vellum became much less popular. The arrival of paper was a major development in book production – and came originally from the Chinese, through the Arabs at the start of the Islamic Golden Age. With the arrival (from the East) of rag paper manufacturing in Europe in the late Middle Ages and the use of the printing press beginning in the mid-fifteenth century, bookbinding began to standardize somewhat, but page sizes still varied considerably. With printing, the books became more accessible and were stored on their side on long shelves for the first time. Clasps were removed, and titles were added to the spine.

Germany became a particular centre of book binding, and by 1729, Leipzig, a prominent centre of the German book-trade (for example), had 20 bookshops, 15 printing establishments, 22 book-binders and three type-foundries in a population of only 28,000 people. The popularity and the increase in affordable books was sustained thereafter, and the bookbinding trade has continued to change and develop into the modern day. It is a branch of industry with intriguing links to learning, academia and culture more generally – and it is hoped that the current reader enjoys this book on the subject.

A NOTE ON BOOKBINDING

A NOTE ON BOOKBINDING.

All owners of libraries have to get books bound from time to time, but comparatively few are able to give clear instructions to their binders. It doubtless saves some trouble if a previously bound volume is sent with a binding order, and the new work simply ordered " to pattern " ; but this habit of sticking to old patterns tends to prevent the binder from improving his work. During the last few years great pains have been taken to improve bookbinding, and it is safe to say that most patterns now in use could be improved upon without increasing their cost.

The work of the Special Committee of the Society of Art on " Leather for Bookbinding " has done much to set standards for good work and good materials, and the report, with its detailed specifications, should prove of great assistance to those who have to give orders for binding books.

Books for binding can be roughly divided into three classes :

1st. Books of value, or of special interest to their owners, that require to be bound as well as the binder can do them.

2nd. Books of permanent interest, but of

Note on Bookbinding.

no special value, that require to be well and strongly bound, but for which the best and most careful work would be too expensive.

3rd. Books of temporary interest that need to be held together and kept neat and tidy for occasional reference.

In other words, some books must be bound as well as possible regardless of expense, some as cheaply as they can be bound well, and others as well as they can be bound cheaply. Rebinding a valuable old book is, at the best, a regrettable necessity, and if its value is to be preserved, the binder must take infinite pains with every detail. Such work should be done entirely by hand, and the binding built up step by step on the book—"made to measure" as it were to suit the needs of the particular volume. Work on which a binder is expected to exercise thought and care on every point must take a long time to do, and therefore must be costly. Cheap binding must be done quickly, and to be done quickly it must be treated "in bulk" without much regard to the requirements of any one book. Up to a point there is no reason why work done quickly should not be done well and strongly, and such work will suit ninety per cent. of books. It is the exceptional book that takes time to bind. The thought that has to be expended on a single binding in the one case, in the other case is given to the first model only; leaving the actual workmen free to work more or less mechanically on repetitions of a model with every detail of which they are familiar.

<small>Note on Bookbinding.</small>

To bind a crown 8vo book ($7\frac{1}{2}" \times 5"$) in full sealskin or morocco of the best quality, carrying out the "Society of Arts" specification I., and doing the work entirely by hand, and as well as it can be done, would cost from 21/- to 25/-, with little or no decoration. If the leaves needed special mending or any sizing or washing, or if the cover were decorated with gold tooling, the cost would be a good deal heavier.

As this is too expensive for the binding of any books but those of value or of special interest to their owners, the binder has to consider what features he can best modify or leave out in order to lessen the cost.

Obviously, the first thing to cut off will be the decoration; next, by making a "half," instead of a "whole," binding about three-quarters of the cost of the leather can be saved. A little more can be saved by mending the backs of the sections a little less neatly, and generally by lowering the standard of finish. By saving in every way, but still working to the specification, perhaps the cost can be halved without taking from the strength of the binding. This gives about 10/6 for the

Note on Bookbinding.
cost of a half-morocco or half-seal binding of a crown 8vo book, sewn flexibly round the bands, and forwarded and lettered by hand. The cost of the best material on such a binding would be about 1/8, and perhaps half of this could be saved by using inferior leather, millboards, etc., but for the sake of 10d. on a half-guinea binding this would be poor economy.

To reduce the cost of binding to this specification much below 10/6 a volume would necessitate a serious and unwarrantable lowering of the standard of work.

Recognising this, the Society of Arts Committee published a second specification for ". Library binding."

To quote from their report:

"This form of binding (Specification I.) must be expensive, as it takes a long time to do. For most books a cheaper form is needed, and after examining and comparing many bindings that had been subjected to considerable use, we have come to the conclusion that the bindings of books sewn on tapes, with 'French' joints, generally fulfil the conditions best.

"The points of advantage claimed for a binding carried out under specification II. are:—

" 1.—It need not be expensive.

"   2.—The construction is sound through-
"   out.
"   3.—A book so bound should open well.
"   4.—The 'French' joint enables com-
"   paratively thick leather to be used.
"   5.—In the absence of raised bands
"   there is no reason for the undue
"   stretching of the leather in covering.
"   6.—The backs of the sections are not
"   injured by saw cuts."

Note on Bookbinding.

By sewing on tapes instead of cords a smooth back is got, which saves time in the working, as it enables the backing to be done in the backing machine. Further time is saved by cutting the edges with the guillotine instead of with the plough; in fact, there is a saving of time at every point.

By substituting machine work for hand work in backing and cutting, and system for thought, the cost of a thoroughly strong half-seal binding for a crown 8vo book can be reduced to about 3/6. This allows of the use of the strongest leather and other sound materials. Further reductions in the price can only be the result of saving a penny here and a penny there, and unless the work is very roughly done, or the materials are inferior, 3/- or 3/6 is as cheap as any odd volume can be bound to this specification. Whole binding in the same style would cost about 8/- for a

Note on Book-binding.

crown 8vo book. In all classes of binding where there are large numbers of volumes of the same size to be bound, the work goes through much more quickly, and therefore more cheaply.

For a cheaper class of work it would be impossible to keep strictly to the specification. To save time the backs of torn sections must be overcast instead of mended, and plates pasted in instead of being guarded.

For the cheapest work, cases are made apart from the books, and cloth is substituted for leather. The weak point in case work is the poorness of the connection between book and binding, but this can be overcome at a very slightly increased cost by sewing on tapes, and using split boards like those used for the "Library Binding." Strong buckram bindings can be made in this way for about 1/6 for a crown 8vo, and if what is known as art-vellum or other cloth is used the cost would be about 3d. less.

When bound books fail to open freely the binder is nearly always blamed for this serious defect, but quite often the fault lies with the choice of paper, which is habitually too thick and stiff for the size of the book. All the binder can do is to get the bend of the leaves as far to the back as possible, and to manage that as few leaves as may be are

Note on Bookbinding.

bent at each opening. If a book is mended at the back instead of overcast, it should open right back to the sewing. If the back is overcast, or "sawn in," a portion of the backs of the leaves is taken up, and so the book cannot open flat.

When possible, and it would be possible in very many cases, it is better to bind "from the sheets." Binders can get unbound copies of books from the publishers, and such books will always be sounder than copies from which the publisher's cases have been removed.

Many modern books are printed on very poor paper. The heavily loaded "Art" paper used for printing half-tone blocks and music upon is perhaps the worst from the binder's point of view. This paper has a surface that readily flakes off, so that anything pasted to it is apt to come away, bringing the surface with it, and as folding breaks the paper at the fold, it cannot be held securely by the sewing thread. This is especially troublesome in the case of music, which must open flat and has to stand more than an ordinary amount of rough usage. Something can be done by strengthening the folds with guards, but this is an operation that adds to the cost of binding.

The following leathers are those in general use for binding books.

Note on Binding Leather.

SEALSKIN.

When properly prepared from the skin of the Greenland seal this leather is most durable and strongly recommended for library work.

PIGSKIN.

This leather is by nature somewhat firm and stiff, and is only suitable for large and heavy books. Skins which have been injured in the process of manufacture, in order to make them soft and easy to work, should not be used.

MOROCCO.

True moroccos are prepared from goatskins. They vary in quality and price. The best "levant" moroccos are prepared from the skins of "Cape goats." Every care should be exercised in selecting suitable skins. No imitations should be used.

SHEEPSKIN, known as Roan, Basil, Skiver, Persian, etc., and often artificially grained and sold as morocco.

Only specially prepared skins of mountain sheep should be used, as they provide a firmer and more durable leather than the skins of the lowland breeds. Although sheepskin is the cheapest leather used for binding, it is, if properly prepared, very serviceable. All sheepskins, however manufactured, should be correctly described.

"Persian" leather should not be used as

although at first mechanically strong, it has little durability.

CALF.

Calfskin is no exception to the general rule that the skins of immature animals are soft and wanting in durability. The early calfskin that has lasted well (15th & 16th Century) shows evidence of considerable growth, and indeed much of it would now be classed as hide.

"Russia," prepared in Russia, should not be used at all, as its method of manufacture renders it a very poor binding leather.

All leathers should be free from mineral acids, and should not be unduly stretched by the leather manufacturer or bookbinder.

It is an elementary rule of craft honesty that materials should look what they are. No leather grained to look like a skin of a better quality should be used, as, apart from the fact that such graining by hot plates is very injurious, the process is, in its nature, a fraudulent one.

Sheepskin should be, frankly, sheepskin, and not bogus morocco or pigskin.

Cloth should be, frankly, a woven material, and not ape the qualities of leather.

Each material has a natural characteristic surface and texture, which a craftsman should respect and make the most of.

Note on Binding. Leather.

HOW TO GIVE ORDERS FOR BINDING.

It is suggested that books for binding should be separated into classes :

By
S. of Arts
Specification.
I.
{ Those that require to be treated individually and are worthy of the best hand work, and whole leather covers. This class of binding can be decorated or not, as desired.

Those that require individual treatment, but are not worth quite the best work, and for which half-binding will be sufficient. }

By
S. of Arts
Specification.
II.
{ The great majority of books that can be treated in bulk. Books of permanent interest to be bound in whole or half-leather binding, "Library style." }

and Books of lesser interest to be bound cheaply in cloth.

It is well to give a binder definite instructions about the treatment of the edges of books. As a rule the edges of books of value are best left entirely uncut, but rough edges on books that are much used are apt to be inconvenient.

Binders are always glad to have a note of the lettering desired for any unusual books, or books in foreign languages, but such notes are quite useless unless they are clearly written.

NOTES ON THE SPECIAL COMMITTEE OF THE SOCIETY OF ARTS ON LEATHER FOR BOOKBINDING.

The Committee appointed by the Society of Arts to investigate the causes that have led to the premature decay of bookbinding leather, consisted of librarians, owners of private libraries, bookbinders, leather sellers leather manufacturers, and leather trades' chemists.

S. of Arts Committee.

The Committee met from time to time under the chairmanship of The Rt. Hon. Viscount Cobham. Most of the actual work was done by two Sub-Committees. "The first of these was to visit a selected number of libraries, and to ascertain the comparative durability of the various bookbinding leathers used at different periods and preserved under different conditions... The second Sub-Committee was appointed to deal with the scientific side of the matter, to ascertain the cause of any deterioration noticed, and, if possible, to suggest methods for its prevention in the future."

The conclusions at which the Committee arrived are summarised in the report as follows :

1. They consider that the general belief that modern bookbinding leather is inferior to

15

S. of Arts Committee. that formerly used, is justified, and that the leather now used for binding books is less durable than that employed fifty years ago, and at previous times. They believe that there ought to be no difficulty in providing leather at the present time as good as any previously made, and they hope that the instructions laid down in the report of the Sub-Committee, printed as Appendix II., will result in the production of such leather.

2. They think that the modern methods of bookbinding are, to some extent, answerable for the lessened permanence of modern bindings. The practice of shaving down thick skins is a fruitful source of deterioration. They think that the adoption of the method of binding recommended in the report of the Sub-Committee, printed as Appendix I., ought to result in a greater permanence of the books treated.

3. They consider that the conditions under which books are best preserved are now fairly well understood, except that the injurious effect of light on leather has not previously been appreciated. They are satisfied that gas fumes are the most injurious of all the influences to which books are subjected. They consider that under proper conditions of ventilation, temperature, and dryness, books may be preserved without deterioration, for

very long periods, on open shelves, but that there is no doubt that, as a general rule, tightly fitting glass cases conduce to their preservation.

S. of Arts Committee.

4. The Committee have satisfied themselves that it is possible to test any leather in such a way as to guarantee its suitability for bookbinding. They have not come to any decision as to the desirability of establishing any formal or official standard, though they consider that this is a point which well deserves future consideration.

The following are the specifications for binding included in the report of the first Sub-Committee :

SPECIFICATION I., FOR BINDING HEAVY OR VALUABLE BOOKS.

SHEETS AND PLATES.	All sheets broken at the back to be made sound with guards. Any single leaves or plates to be guarded round adjoining sections. Folded plates to be guarded with linen at folds. No pasting-on to be allowed.	*Specification for binding heavy or valuable books.*

Specification for binding heavy or valuable books.

END PAPERS. End papers not to be pasted on or overcast, but to be made with stout linen joint and sewn on as a section. Some system of folding or zigzaging which allows a little play without danger of breaking away is advocated. End papers to be made of good paper.

SEWING. Sewing to be flexible, round the bands and all along the sections. Thread to be unbleached linen, and bands to be of stout hempen cord and at least five in number.

BOARDS. To be of best black millboard. The edge of the millboard in the joint to be slightly rounded.

LACING IN SLIPS. All five slips to be laced into each board and not reduced unduly. It would be better to sink places in the board to receive the slips than to weaken them by injudicious fraying out.

Specification for binding heavy or valuable books.

CUTTING EDGES. This will depend on the librarian's orders.

HEADBANDS. Headbands to be worked on stout cord, vellum, or catgut, with very frequent tie-downs, and to be firmly set with stout brown paper, linen or leather.

LINING UP. If it is necessary to line up the back it is best done with leather or linen, leather for preference.

COVERING. Leather not to be unduly pared down and not made very wet before covering. Care to be taken not to stretch the leather more than necessary. No hollow backs to be used, but the leather to be attached to the back.

LEATHER. See report of Sub-Committee. [Leather to be free from mineral acids, and generally treated as recommended in the Sub-Committee's report.]

Specification for binding heavy or valuable books.

HANDLES FOR PULLING OUT OF SHELF. In the case of very large books that are likely to be much used, it is advisable to have a strap of leather going loosely across the back and each end fastened to a board of the book. The Sub-Committee saw some such arrangement at one or two of the libraries visited, and it seemed that a great saving of the binding resulted from the use.

Note that manuscripts on vellum, or books of special value will, of course, require bindings designed to meet the special conditions.

Specification for ordinary library binding.

SPECIFICATION II., FOR ORDINARY LIBRARY BINDING.

SHEETS AND PLATES. All sheets broken at the back to be made sound with guards, any single leaves or plates to be guarded round adjoining sections. Folded plates to be guarded with linen at folds. No pasting-on to be allowed.

		Specification for ordinary library binding.
END PAPERS.	To be of good paper sewn on. No pasting-on or overcasting to be allowed.	
SEWING.	To be on not less than four unbleached linen tapes, with unbleached linen thread of suitable thickness. Books to be glued up and backed in the ordinary way, or left square.	
BOARDS.	To be made "split boards" like those vellum binders use. Straw board lined with a thick black board liner.	
CUTTING	or treatment of edges. To depend on orders.	
ATTACHING SLIPS.	Slips to be pasted on to waste end papers which should be cut off about two inches from the back and inserted with slips in the centre of split board. The board to be left about $\frac{1}{8}''$ from the back of the book to form a French joint.	

Specification for ordinary library binding.	HEAD-BAND-ING.	Headbands to be worked on round cord or gut with frequent tie-downs, so as to be able to bear the strain of the books being taken from the shelf, or in cases where the expenses of a worked headband is thought to be too great, a piece of string may be inserted into the fold of the leather at the head or tail.
	COVER-ING.	Leather not to be unduly pared down. The French joint should make it possible to use far thicker leather han is usual. As there are no raised bands on the back the leather need not be unduly stretched in covering. For small books leather from comparatively small skins that will need but little paring should be selected.

These extracts are quoted from the preliminary report published in 1901. It is understood that the committee's final report, based on some four years' work, will be issued early in 1905.

www.ingramcontent.com/pod-product-compliance
Lightning Source LLC
LaVergne TN
LVHW041313080426
835510LV00009B/973